The New Reality of International Telecommunications Strategy

Robert C. Fonow

Center for Technology and National Security Policy

National Defense University

January 2006

The views expressed in this report are those of the authors and do not reflect the official policy or position of the National Defense University, the Department of Defense, or the U.S. Government. All information and sources for this paper were drawn from unclassified materials.

Robert C. Fonow is managing director of RGI, Ltd, www.rgiltd.com.

Defense & Technology Papers are published by the National Defense University Center for Technology and National Security Policy, Fort Lesley J. McNair, Washington, DC. CTNSP publications are available online at http://www.ndu.edu/ctnsp/publications.html.

Contents

1. Introduction

Until recently, the United States was the undisputed leader in all aspects of international telecommunications operations and innovation. The United States was the progenitor of the undersea cable infrastructure and satellite system, and American companies led the advancement of commercial global telecommunications networks. The United States was the hub of the Internet, the best known sub-network of the international telecommunications system. Today, though, Internet hubs are being replicated in several geographical regions.[1] More importantly, every major American telecommunications company has retreated extensively from the ownership of fundamental international network assets. This has important strategic implications for American defense communications, logistics, commerce, and diplomacy.

The international telecommunications system is in transition from U.S. dominance to distributed, regional dominance. Europe has become the first continent with its own complete and integrated hub to provide services for Internet customers on a technical basis equal to the United States; more bandwidth exists between European cities than between Europe and the United States. Intra-regional links between Asian networks, particularly China's telecommunications expansion beyond the mainland, are progressing quickly, and interest is growing in inter-regional links between Europe, Russia, China, and the Middle East, which would form the first stage of Eurasian telecommunications integration. Within five to ten years, the United States will be only one of several regional telecommunications centers, and not necessarily the most powerful and influential.

China is becoming the greatest regional competitor to U.S. network interests, producing its own chip designs, software and protocols, commercial applications, and, eventually, military tactics based on these innovations. This rise may be augmented by Indian and Russian intellectual resources, as well as those from numerous transnational corporations, many of them headquartered in the United States.

The United States is the relative leader in telecommunications today, but the relationships are changing quickly. Microsoft, Oracle, and Intel are likely to remain world technical leaders, but American commercial success and military dominance, which increasingly depends on dominance in networking technology, are being undermined by several developments:

- Rapidly increasing technical expertise in countries and societies as diverse as China, India, Russia, Israel, Eastern Europe, and the European Community.

- Transfer of commercial technologies and outsourcing of their manufacture, which puts the United States outside many of the main threads of technical and services innovation.

- Education demographics that indicate that the United States will be only one of several equally innovative countries within ten years. Numerous statistics suggest enrollments in

---

[1] "Global Internet Geography 2005 Executive Summary, Primedia Corp." www.telegeography.com/ee/free_resources/gig2005_exec_sum-01.php

university-level technological education of approximately 2.5 million students in China, 2.4 million in Russia, 1.9 million in India, and 1.7 million in the United States.[2] Each of these countries has world-class centers of excellence and relationships with centers of excellence in other countries. A diffused international telecommunications system has accelerated the spread of knowledge.

- The capability of competitive nations to develop "leapfrog technologies" in international telecommunications. Some of these technologies have the capacity to constrain the capability of the United States to maintain commercial and military supremacy, especially in network-centric warfare.[3]

American leadership is particularly threatened in the telecommunications technologies that make up the underlying routing and protocol fabric of the Internet. Countries capable of challenging the United States have invested heavily in networks. China in particular has a network infrastructure that is as good in its critical cores as the current American telecommunication system and shows every possibility of surpassing it in the next several years. In fact, potential competitors already have surpassed the United States in many ways in the use of the new technologies in commercial applications, as anyone familiar with wireless-handset development and use in Japan, Korea, and China knows.

This paper considers the relative decline of American telecommunications leadership from geopolitical and technical perspectives. This decline is important to recognize and understand because it is masked by the achievements of the American economy and U.S. military successes since the end of the Cold War.[4]

The five sections of this paper cumulatively describe the present situation and its likely development over the next 10–15 years. Section one explores current perceptions of potential technological competitors and adversaries and discusses development philosophies and technical advancement in telecommunications in China and, to a lesser extent, Russia and India.

Section two analyzes some of the major factors that have made China America's biggest telecommunications competitor, including centralized state planning, technology transfer, the development of the Chinese microprocessor industry, and the Chinese takeover of global telecommunications hardware engineering. Software development in China, a more recent emphasis of the Chinese government, also is addressed.

---

[2] In telecommunications system operations, these numbers do not include the high number of adjunct technicians running billing systems, network-monitoring facilities, and provisioning systems necessary to run a modern complex national telecommunications capability.

[3] This is a paper about geopolitics, not a primer on network-centric warfare, an area in which fluid definitions can be applied to warfare on strategic, operational, and tactical levels. Wherever possible, I use the term *telecommunications-based warfare* because I think the term *network-centric warfare* is too closely associated with the Internet conceived as a global, unitary network. Telecommunications-based warfare does not depend entirely on the Internet. For example, if the Internet were to experience a catastrophic failure during naval actions near the coast of China, significant command and control could be accomplished with high-frequency radios and specialized modems. Older technology is sometimes the most robust.

[4] Peter J. Hugill, *Global Communications since 1844,* (Baltimore and London: The Johns Hopkins University Press, 1999).

Section three briefly examines the process of financing technological development in China. State-supported finance and access to private equity are related to models of research, innovation, and product development in the Chinese telecommunications industry.

Section four discusses Chinese emphasis on developing a leading position in IPv6—the underlying protocol of the next-generation Internet and a potential leapfrog technology—and concludes that China is integrating IPv6 technologies into a new political economy that is consistent with Chinese goals for regional economic and political dominance.

Section five suggests the possibility that China, based on its demographics, educational resources, and recent rapid progress, will surpass the United States in technological innovation in telecommunications. Among other consequences, this development threatens America's increasingly network-based defense strategy.

The paper does not argue that the United States will necessarily become a victim of other countries' successes, but it does suggest the need for greater awareness of the growing technical power, particularly in telecommunications, of economic competitors and potential adversaries. To paraphrase a leading geopolitical thinker of another age, Halford Mackinder, "Information is power, and whoever rules the world's telecommunications system commands the world."

2. International Telecommunications

Perceptions

In a recent report, The International Telecommunications Union (ITU) describes a future of constant global innovation and growth, particularly in telecommunications services and the increasingly small and mobile access devices that will drive the industry.[5] Virtually all manufacturing of these devices will be in China. The Chinese telecommunications industry will service the most dynamic new markets as more people around the world integrate low-cost telecommunications into their daily activities. More engineers and technologists, especially in China, India, and Europe, will gain an understanding of the underlying technology, and more and more capital will follow the highest returns in intellectual capacity at lowest cost. Several countries will approach parity with the U.S. in telecommunications technology innovation in the next ten years.

This means the pace of international technical innovation will accelerate. Already the rate of change is so fast it is impossible to get a fix on the status of networks in transition. It is only possible to get a fix on perceptions, or misperceptions, which develop and change more slowly.

One common misperception is that there is a global telecommunications network. This is not quite precise. There is an international system of telecommunications that corresponds with the international system of states. In the international telecommunications system, including the Internet, applications such as financial transactions, web searches, and email are operated on a meta-idea of globalization but rely on a physical set of private networks owned by businesses and governments within sovereign states. So, at every level of strategic and commercial interconnection, this global network is as much competitive as cooperative.

Another common misperception is that the United States somehow controls this non-existent global telecommunications network. Much of the world's network infrastructure is really owned by businesses and governments of other countries. Virtually every American telecommunications operating company has retreated from active ownership of international telecommunications networks.[6] This is not simply a matter of ceding commercial dominance: it has implications for U.S. military operations. In periods of high traffic, which often accompany a crisis, it is estimated that up to 90 percent of Department of Defense (DOD) traffic is carried on networks owned and maintained by entities in other countries.[7] These countries have the capacity to inhibit or disrupt U.S. telecommunications outside American borders at any time.

---

[5] "The Portable Internet," International Telecommunications Union, Geneva, September 2004.

[6] The last American international telecommunications company with its own assets around the world, the Los Angeles-based Infonet Services Company, was sold to British Telecommunications PLC in May 2005.

[7] Lawrence Greenberg, "Danger.com: National Security in a Wired World", in Economic Strategy and National Security: A Next Generation Approach, ed. Patrick J. DeSouza (Boulder, CO: Westview Press, 2000. It's impossible to put a precise figure on the amount of military traffic passing through international networks at any time. A recent

Still another misperception is that the United States maintains and will continue to maintain technological leadership in telecommunications technologies. While the United States might still be considered the global technological leader, it is unlikely to maintain this position. Western Europe, China, India, and Russia, either alone or in bilateral or multilateral combinations, have the capability to match or exceed the United States in specific areas of telecommunications innovation. The telecommunications manufacturing industry has almost entirely moved to China and, therefore, is substantially controlled by China.

The following sections explore several of the issues surrounding telecommunications geopolitics and technology innovation in the United States, China, Russia, and India.

China

It is widely believed in the United States that China does the low-end manufacturing and the United States operates in the higher reaches of the economic value chain, doing the thinking, design, systems integration, and selling. However, China already has the components in place to become the most sophisticated telecommunications society on the planet in the next ten years. It already possesses the world's largest fiber optic networks, cellular and mobile networks, national Internet, terrestrial access networks, third- and fourth-generation test beds (3G and 4G cellular networks with high speed data capacity), and telecommunication manufacturing capability.

The U.S.-China Economic and Security Review Commission, mandated by Congress to produce annual reports on U.S.-China relations, is concerned that as China's economic power expands, its ability to acquire advanced U.S. technology and production facilities will increase exponentially. Unfortunately that only considers part of the problem. China is eclectic in its pursuit of technology. The United States is not its only target: China applies the same strategies to collect technological know-how to every country with a developed technical infrastructure.[8]

What does all this mean? According to John Gage, a leading American technologist and Sun Microsystem's Chief Technology Officer, it means China is becoming an innovative competitor via a "technology explosion."[9]

> In China, the last five years have seen an incredible explosion of innovation and experimentation, as the Chinese Education and Research Network (CerNet) has linked a thousand universities, courses teaching Java to millions of students have proliferated, and a new generation of companies such as Huawei and UT Starcom[10] have emerged as world competitors in networking and distributed systems.

---

figure puts the amount at 70% for a major U.S. international exercise. Appendix A, page CRS-34, "Network Centric Warfare: Background and Oversight Issues for Congress," Clay Wilson, March 18, 2005.

[8] U.S.-China Economic and Security Review Commission, Annual Report, June 2004.

[9] China's "Technology Explosion," John Gage, *Red Herring*, May 15, 2004.

[10] UT Starcom is in fact a U.S.-based company, but most of its production and sales are in Asia.

Because innovations are inevitable when you have a large group working in technology areas, as China has, the impact of CerNet will be considerable. The connection linking Chinese universities is now at 10 gigabits between some campuses, and it reaches out to tens of millions of Chinese students and faculty.[11] Add to that the explosion of the wireless network, with nearly 300 million mobile users in China, and you have a caldron right now: a center of innovation that is supported by very inexpensive telecommunications

China has standardized on open source, with Linux as a core component, and we're going to see a round of innovations in provision of mobile services that require high bandwidth because China now has it. When you visit any university, you find a hardworking and dedicated group of students. And enrollments in science and engineering are rising, in contrast to the U.S.

It's true of all high-tech companies in the United States; if you analyze the work force you'll find 10, 20, maybe even 30 percent are of Chinese origins, with strong links back to their university on the mainland. If you examine the technical journals, like the 30 or so published by IEEE, you will notice the number of articles published by Chinese has gone up by a factor of 10 over the past four to five years. These are peer-reviewed, high quality, advanced engineering journals. I think the last five years have transformed the interaction of Chinese engineering with the rest of the world.

Couple this rate of innovation with the increasing Chinese and international capital resources being allocated to applied research in China, and the seriousness of the potential competition becomes apparent. The investment growth curve in science and technology appears to be accelerating. Extrapolation from information available from the Chinese Ministry of Science and Technology yields an estimate of $33 billion in 2005, growing at approximately 25 percent a year.

China's Commercial Strategy
As always in a large bureaucracy, where one sits shapes ones views. The Departments of Commerce and State view China as a necessary and manageable commercial partner. The U.S. Trade Representative and Department of Defense see a strategic competitor and, eventually, a threat to the United States in both trade and military affairs. Americans tend to think we drive events. Actually, U.S. government perceptions and actions have been largely irrelevant to China's takeover of the telecommunications industry.

At the United States and China Telecommunications Summit, June 17, 2004, Secretary of Commerce Evans described the United States and China as the world's primary engines of global telecommunications growth. Such statements are flattering to the Chinese and always result in appreciative smiles and nods all around. In return, as in most conferences, Chinese commercial and government leaders acknowledged that the United States is the global technical leader and is likely to remain so for a long time. Based on my personal experience in China, this is universally stated by every technical leader at almost every meeting with foreigners. But it is becoming

---

[11] U.S.-China Economic and Security Review Commission, "China as an Emerging Regional and Technology Power: Implications for U.S. Economic and Security interests", Greg Lucier, testimony on February 12–13, 2004

apparent that no one in the Chinese technical or political leadership believes it any more, especially for the middle or long term.

No sense of threat or confrontation is evident in a commercial conference sponsored by the Department of Commerce. It is a collaborative meeting of engineers, scientists, and academics interested in the general promotion of technical knowledge and the economic benefits that can be derived from it. The meetings are always collegial and friendly. Information is freely and usually condescendingly offered by U.S. participants to the Chinese. Both sides openly discuss national industrial policy. But the alert participant will notice clear cultural differences in approaching telecommunications development and may begin to understand how China has advanced so quickly in so many areas.

Even in the era of the socialist market economy, China maintains significant elements of a planned command economy. [12] Although state planning is antithetical to the free market model by which many Westerners judge the Chinese economy, it works in many sectors, including telecommunications.

The Chinese have used several methods to reach their current high standard of telecommunication development.

- Extensively detailed Communist Party Five-Year Plans that are a pivot of the national industrial policy for telecommunications.

- A restrictive regulatory policy that prevents foreign operators from competing with indigenous operating companies, such as China Telecom and China Netcom, thereby providing closed markets for Chinese equipment suppliers.

- Joint ventures and wholly owned foreign enterprises that bring sophisticated technology to China in return for market access.

- A system of university-affiliated enterprises that provide state-funded research for industry, a funding system that developed when companies had very little access to capital. This relieves corporations of the financial burden of R&D and permits the government to allocate innovation to select enterprises. These operations are focused mostly on technology transfer and product development. As of mid-2002, there were over 5,000 enterprises of all types affiliated with Chinese universities.

- Government-to-government foreign cooperation agreements with the United States, Russia, India, Israel, and several other European and Asian countries.

---

[12] In many ways the current Chinese economy can be explained by a reference to Lenin's New Economic Policy, a state capitalist model dominated by democratic centralism, except that under Deng Xiao Ping the ideas and structure had time to mature. The idea that China is emerging into unfettered free-market capitalism and eventual popular democracy strikes me as unfounded in Chinese history or culture.

- Education of Chinese engineers abroad, who then return with new knowledge. Many work for the newest and most innovative Chinese information technology (IT) companies.

- Commercial espionage.[13]

- Sophisticated collection programs of publicly available research publications and web-based research.

- Internally generated innovation, R&D centers, and research parks. The Zhonguancun high-tech zone in Beijing is reported to have 10,000 companies, though most of them are quite small and often employ only a handful of people. Only 12 percent of these companies are foreign owned. Technical zones in Shanghai and Guangdong province provide China with a diverse, regionalized, technical base, each zone increasingly producing technical innovation.

- Large-scale piracy, which continues to characterize intellectual property rights (IPR) protection in China and is a major concern for U.S. exporters of high-tech goods and services. While the central government has instituted laws to strengthen IPR protection, enforcement has suffered from a lack of government coordination and from local protectionism and corruption.

The American style of planning and funding technological development is largely iterative. It is based on a relationship between funding and market results. Virtually all economic growth in the American economy, and indeed all industrial economies, comes from incremental improvement in productivity, products, and markets, not from exciting new enterprises and businesses based on radical new technologies. In the United States, telecommunications funding is conservative and goal driven. Capital is invested with a goal to maximize return on investment within the existing telecommunications technological and regulatory structure. Products like iPod and Blackberry, while commercially successful in the United States, are considered to be behind the design curve in leading Chinese companies.[14]

The sources of new industries and new commercial opportunities come from radical market- and technology-based innovations that create markets.[15] Technical innovation often comes from the interaction of talented communities of engineers and scientists. And almost all the conditions that were present in Silicon Valley in the 1990s, a period of intense innovation in the United States, are present in Beijing and Shanghai today.

Until very recently, and despite some similarities to the American model, Chinese technology development derived from a different philosophical orientation. The Chinese science and technology community has a deep interest in understanding the historical dynamics of

---

[13] Trade Secrets Law Forum, www.rmarkhalligan2.com maintains an active bulletin board on trade secrets and commercial espionage, including Chinese activities.
[14] Many of the early developments in packet switching and other telecommunications derived from military research.
[15] Executive Summary, "U.S.-China Seminar on Technical Innovations," George Mason University, Summer 2002.

technology development. Perhaps this is a residual Marxist component of Chinese technical thought; if there is a component of historical determinism in technology development, knowing how it works could save a lot of time and money.

Of course, this will change as a new generation of technologists, often trained in American universities, becomes ascendant. And it became apparent in 2005 that the Chinese are indeed incorporating a more iterative model into the socialist market economy. *Thus, the country is combining the advantages of a command economy, which gives a national priority to telecommunications development, and the iterative, intellectual processes and growing funding capabilities of a Western development model.* In a number of telecommunications technologies, the Chinese have moved quickly from imitation to incremental design improvements, to indigenous innovation. This is evident in the evolution of technological capability in such Chinese telecommunications companies as EastCom, Huawei, and China Putian, which are large, export-oriented telecommunications system manufacturers[16]

India

Until recently, India, as a putative neutral country, was on the margins of U.S. interests. In the last several years, as India's software development capabilities and growing regional influence have become increasingly evident, American interest has grown.

India has a highly developed technical capability that is different from China's. India's technical plan appears to be market driven, providing low-cost, advanced, software-support services to multinational companies. There is no indication yet that India is interested in becoming a global leader in the development of telecommunications manufacturing and services standards, which is a goal of China. Current estimates indicate national telecommunications and IT revenues at between $14 and $17 billion. This is important, because telecommunications and IT are so closely intertwined in India. The applications that run on the physical infrastructure of the international telecommunication system, and the back office functions, such as billing, order entry, maintenance scheduling, fault reporting, are IT functions. These are functions that can be modularized and resold, therefore are dependent on excellent administrative management, a practice that Indian companies like Wipro and Infosys have mastered.

The industry has been highly export-oriented since the first leased lines (privately purchased portions of circuits) between the United State and India were used for software development in the mid-1980s at Carnegie-Mellon University. Domestic demand accounts for less than one-fifth of output. IT products—mainly software—accounted for 11 percent of current-account receipts and 19 percent of goods exports in 2002/2003. The most important market is the United States, which absorbs about 60 percent of India's software exports.[17]

India has several major privatized telecom groups. The most significant are the Tata Group, which is almost wholly domestic, and the Reliance Group, which is particularly aggressive in

---

[16] Robert Fonow, "Beyond the Mainland: Chinese Telecommunications Expansion," *Defense Horizons* 29, (Washington, DC: Center for Technology and National Security Policy, July 2003)
[17] Economist Intelligence Unit Viewswire, New York, Jan 13, 2004

India and internationally. Reliance Infocomm, owned by the Reliance group (which is controlled by the Ambani family, India's largest business group) is building an 85,000-kilometer, fiber-optic network linking 750 towns and cities. The network is part of a $3 billion investment in Reliance Infocomm in the past two years. It is designed to service the data needs of broadband customers and is currently used mainly for Reliance's fixed-line and mobile telephony applications. Reliance has over 25 million cellular subscribers.

India missed out on the bandwidth boom of the late 1990s, which put vast international capacity across the Atlantic and Pacific but left India relatively isolated. This is changing rapidly. According to Telegeography, India's international submarine capacity will have grown from 31 Gbps in 2001 to 541 Gbps by the end of 2004. This is still a minor percentage of global bandwidth, but if a company or government is sending traffic to South Asia, it will go over Indian owned and managed telecommunications resources, an important geopolitical consideration.

In January 2004 the Reliance group completed the acquisition of the globe-spanning FLAG undersea cable system, and in March 2004 announced a new cable project between the Middle East and India. The new cable system, called FALCON, will provide 15 terabits of capacity from Egypt and around the Gulf in a self-healing network that will link to India and Hong Kong and China by 2005. Tata Group recently announced the acquisition of Tycom's submarine cable assets. Indian companies now own and control a major undersea fiber-optic sector of the South Asian telecommunications infrastructure linking the Middle East and Singapore.

Bandwidth capacity prices from the United States to India are still five to ten times higher than on the U.S.-Hong Kong route. The increase in capacity and number of competing cable systems will drive down the price of bandwidth to India, making Indian software development even cheaper for American and European corporations. Elsewhere in Asia, prices declined by 60 percent or more in the last year. This decline is likely to be repeated in India, which will make the country an even stronger competitor for outsourced labor from the United States and Europe.

India now controls the flow of telecommunications traffic in South Asia.[18] It should not be considered a client of the United States. At the Global Strategic Review of the International Institute for Strategic Studies in Geneva in September 2005, very senior Indian officials were explicit that India would keep a balanced approach to politics, diplomacy, and commerce with both China and the United States, specifically stating the United States would not be able to use its relationships with India to counterbalance Chinese interests. In 2005 there emerged dramatic growth in the cooperation between Chinese and Indian telecommunications equipment suppliers and software developers.[19]

Russia

---

[18] See www.telegeography.com, free resources, maps for an indication of traffic flows in South Asia and the Middle East.
[19] Howard W. French, "India and China woo cross-border business", International Herald Tribune (New York Times), November 8, 2005.

The Soviet Union was an early competitor with the United States in telecommunications switching technologies but eventually lagged behind. Currently, Russia has no major international competitor companies in the telecommunications equipment sector. However, it does have numerous smaller manufacturing and assembly companies in the router and ancillary networking equipment markets that produce capable products. Some bilateral research, sponsored by China Putian, Huawei, and ZTE corporations, is being conducted between Chinese and Russian telecommunications research institutes, but on a scale that is not likely to result in leapfrog technologies.

The Russian telecom press continues to register disappointment that Russia, for all of its remarkable engineering talent, lags behind China and India in telecommunications and software development. A predicted breakthrough as a primary destination for outsourcing didn't happen. This is a consequence of the structure of the telecommunications and information technologies in the country. India has been a code-writing shop, selling low-cost, routine software services by the hour. Russian programmers are hardware and system integration engineers, often trained to work on massive, complex projects involving the country's energy industry and the space and military sectors. As a consequence, Russia can't compete with the Indian outsourcing sector for routine coding, which is basically a rote, organizational model. Some Russian technologists believe that their future lies with product development (the Israeli model) rather than offshore-contracted programming (the Indian model).[20]

The best prospects for Russian software are related to product-oriented and system-integration business models rather than order-oriented man-hours sold at the lowest cost. For example, the Russian company SPIRIT licenses furnished software products to Japan Radio Corporation, NEC, Nortel, Samsung, Texas Instruments, Toshiba, and other leaders of international computer and telecommunications markets. In 2001, SPIRIT entered into a strategic relationship with Texas Instruments (TI) for the largest, licensed, software export deal in Russian history. The market-leading TI C54 Digital Signal Processor (DSP) has SPIRIT's integrated telephony software embedded in the processor. The DSPs are included in cell phones, wireless access systems, fax machines, modems, personal digital assistants, etc. for major suppliers around the world.[21] With access to capital and a clearly developed strategy, Russian companies can be innovative and service the largest international technology companies. But this is rare.

Russia has a legacy of advanced education, including one of the highest literacy rates in the world, a tradition of high-tech research and development, competitiveness, and mathematical skills. Russian software executives believe that quality is higher in Russia than in India and that labor costs are lower. Some analysts believe that the world's best—and also cheapest—programmers are in Russia. Russia's software industry lacks brand value, management, and marketing expertise, but clearly has the capability to make rapid advances under better management and with access to capital. Some of the obstacles to progress are lack of interaction between companies for fear of poaching employees, language barriers (e.g. relatively few technicians with good English skills), and outdated management techniques. In addition, training, education, and R&D in software are at low levels.

---

[20] The comparison of "the Israeli model" and "the Indian model" is the shorthand description used by Russian telecommunications writers.
[21] Mr. Sviridenko's interview is on www.outsourcing-Russia.com, accessed on August 27, 2004.

High-tech corridors are emerging in and between St. Petersburg, Moscow, and Novosibirsk. Geopolitically this means a path of industrial production and trading along the old Silk Road and the reemergence of a sophisticated line of commercial centers from Shanghai to Madrid. U.S. exports to Russia totaled only $2.5 billion in 2003, up 2.2 percent over the previous year. That makes Russia the 38th-ranked market for American goods. Russia exports to the United States totaled about $8.6 billion in 2003—up 25 percent, mainly because of a rise in energy prices.[22] Growth will come from Eurasian economic interaction, and Russian companies will provide the IT and telecommunications that bridge the continent.

Today, the telecommunications and information technology businesses in Russia display uneven signs of stability and progress. Certainly in Russia's favor is that in the Dot Com era it didn't over invest in telecoms.[23] As a result, the country is seen as a good destination for development capital. A surge in the flow to Russia of unsecured loans insured by the European Credit Agency (ECS) is underway, mainly for large investments in telecommunications. Russian telecom companies will borrow more than $500 million under ECA guarantees this year. MTS is seeking bids from banks for a mandate to raise up to $350 million. Vimplecom, the other big player, is expected to borrow a similar amount, and Megafon is in talks with banks for a $150 million transaction. To finance telecommunication network rollouts, ECA-backed loans are the cheapest available to Russian borrowers.[24]

In telecommunications, Russia is served by several large, competing operating companies and is unique among modern countries in the remoteness of much of the country in relation to a relatively small population. As a consequence, in contrast to WLAN/Wi-Fi development common in Western Europe, new services in Russia are pushing newer technologies like WiMax, or Wi-Fi networks engineered to have some of the range of WiMax, capable of supporting 70Mbits per second date rates at a typical range of up to 30 miles. WiMax has the potential to complete the infrastructure buildup within Russia, where as many as 50,000 villages don't have widely available phone service.[25]

Russian telecommunications is at an inflection point. The industry has the potential to develop sophisticated, value-added services and could be the leader in long-range, wide-bandwidth wireless applications. But the country must overcome a number of problems including corruption, capital allocation to promising industries, and improvement of management and financial reporting.

Chapter Summary

What is happening in China, and to a lesser extent in India, is the internationalization of knowledge being reflected back at the United States. The American companies operating in the

---

[22] Alan M. Field, *Journal of Commerce*, April 26, 2004, 1.

[23] John Waggoner and Sandra Block, "Where in the world are today's hottest markets," *USA Today*, April 5, 2004.

[24] Simon Pirani, "Through the Looking Glass," *Trade Finance*, April 2004.

[25] EBN, "Russia's weak IT base draws investors…..", Nicolas Mokhoff, Manhasset, NY, Nov 24, 2003, p.4, now known as Electronics Supply & Manufacturing, www.my-esm.com, published by CMP group.

market economic system have sold or traded their intellectual property to any bidder that could lower manufacturing cost and maximize profits. The intellectual output of large cadres of Indian and Chinese engineers, trained in American companies, and at taxpayer expense at publicly supported universities and research institutes, is now being arrayed against us—with unknown and unpredictable consequences.

Today, China is the optimal country for manufacturing telecommunications equipment, including Internet and other data communications equipment. China can design and produce equipment from chip level up. As equipment gets smaller, and profitability is based on highly customized products, China will become the main source of new product development while remaining the key manufacturing country for global markets. This is because it possesses a vast supply of highly educated and cheap technical labor.

India is a production line for low-cost coding but will move up the value chain. However, because it doesn't have a manufacturing base, the software it produces is used on equipment and systems produced elsewhere, and it will probably always be a secondary source of innovation, primarily focused on support software functions.

Russia is not yet a competitor on the scale of China and India. Russia can develop into a formidable technical innovator very quickly with access to capital, improved management training, and open access to markets in the telecommunications industry. The country possesses all the tools to be a leader in telecommunications technology and software development. Its under-utilized intellectual resources are vast, and significant numbers of scientists and engineers are world class. Thousands of Russian engineers have experience in large-scale program management. This skilled workforce is largely underemployed and poorly paid.

My recent experience in telecommunications development in Russia in 2004 and 2005 suggests a market that is still struggling to find its place in the global competitive system. There is an inertia and resistance to process change in Russia that does not exist in the United States, China, and India. There is a very real question whether existing regulatory and management structures will permit the imagination and entrepreneurialism necessary for success as cellular networks reach saturation in Russia, and further growth and profits in mobile, land line, and fixed wireless depends on the development of value-added services. The heavy hand of bureaucracy and political favoritism, combined with a prideful sense among many Russian managers that Western or Chinese management practices have little relevance to Russia, is a continuing drag on IT and telecommunications development, especially beyond metropolitan Moscow.

In summary, the United States is not the unassailable leader in telecommunications equipment and services any longer. India has strengths in software development and outsourcing. Russia has strengths in large-scale system integration and long-range, high-bandwidth networking. But China is the most important competitor, a thriving hybrid model of capitalism and command-economy planning, with impressively growing technical resources. The next sections examine the factors that make China such a current and future telecom power.

3. Changing Structures of Telecommunications Production: The Emerging Dominance of China

Overview

China has a unique combination of competitive advantages: a booming market for electronics products and services; the world's largest pool of low-cost, specialized, and easily retrainable skills; the emergence of sophisticated lead users and test-bed markets; the ability of government policymakers to learn from the achievements and mistakes of Japan, Korea, and Taiwan; and the ability to quickly adjust its own national and local policies. In the past few years, China has experienced explosive growth in IT exports and is now the third largest IT exporter (up from tenth in 2000). The production of these exports is highly concentrated in a few clusters in the Pearl River Delta, the Yangtze River Delta, and Beijing. The location-specific advantages of these clusters shape China's overall technological trajectory, as well as the development of its innovative capabilities. [26] These developments indicate a profound change in international competitive telecommunications relations.

Chinese government officials believe the United States and Japan reached their leading positions in the IT manufacturing industry because they were able to grasp and monopolize the design of integrated circuits and key components. Therefore, strengthening the development of core technologies, especially in the design and production of integrated components, became vital in the coordination between manufacturing and service industries in China.[27]

In this process, foreign telecom firms have been required to provide substantial financing, telecom equipment, and know-how as part of Sino-foreign technology transfer in return for access to sales channels. Until very recently, most American companies gained market access in relation to the amount of technology transferred to China. The Chinese purpose is to get not the equipment, but the know-how that comes with making the equipment. This explains why the value of a joint venture has been measured according to the level of human resources that Western companies send to the venture in China to expedite technology transfer.

Fiber grids and next-generation telecommunications networks, with their intellectual genesis abroad, are installed in every Chinese province. China has numerous telecom R&D labs funded by the Chinese government whose role is to integrate, adapt, and test foreign equipment that is to be connected to the national network—and to imitate and improve these technologies, often through reverse engineering. As a consequence, China now produces domestically developed fiber optic cables, telecommunications switches, and routers that compete with foreign-made

---

[26] Dieter Ernst and Barry Naughton, "China's Emerging Industrial Economy, Insights from the IT Industry", Paper for East-West Center Conference on China's Emerging Capitalist System, August 10-12, 2005. This is an up-to-date and comprehensive analysis of the nature of the Chinese IT industry.

[27] 10–Year Plan and Long Range Plan 3.1.6, Chinese University of Hong Kong translation of Chinese Version, provided by APCO China

brands in China. Huawei commands the greatest market share in the PRC for optical systems equipment, outselling Lucent and Alcatel. Huawei's Cisco-look-alike routers sell around the world at 50 percent of the price of comparable Cisco equipment.

R&D in China now is sufficiently robust to develop communications systems and the software to run them. R&D activity includes integrating foreign technology with local systems and making foreign technology compatible with Chinese technical standards.[28] This latter form of knowledge transfer (systems and standards integration capabilities) in particular could be useful to China's defense modernization goals, especially in telecommunications command and control systems.

The two most important technologies of China's pursuit of a leading position in global telecommunications are semiconductors and software. Both industries have benefited from a concerted Chinese government effort to bolster the country's competitive position.

Semiconductors

Semiconductors are the foundation technology of modern telecommunications equipment. They are the microprocessors or computer chips that execute the software commands that drive the system. In the semiconductor sector, U.S. government analysts judge China now to be at most two years behind leading American semiconductor manufacturing technology—and only one generation behind the commercial state of the art, and closing fast. A significant percentage of global semiconductor production now resides in China. More companies are placing their design and production in Asia, particularly in China, a development that will only hasten China's telecommunications rise. Several structural changes in the semiconductor industry are facilitating and encouraging this shift.

Physical proximity of intellectual assets is considered vital to innovative chip design, a process that creates the greatest value in the electronics and telecommunications industries. In research related to the semiconductor industry, Keith Pavitt distinguished cognitive and organizational dimensions of technological complexity. As for the cognitive dimension, a chip is "made up of numerous components and subsystems whose interactions are often non-linear and therefore impossible to predict." Therefore the closer the interaction among key developers working in close proximity, the more likely something useful will result from theory. One can deduce from this that the more the semiconductor industry concentrates in Asia, the more innovative ideas will emerge there.[29]

Dieter Ernst, an evolutionary economist at the University of Hawaii East West Center, argues that chip design is moving to Asia in direct response to design methodology changes (system-level integration through modular design and new organization of automated "design factories"). Both changes have dramatically increased the cognitive and organizational complexity of design. This makes it less likely that a single company will exclusively handle all stages of the design of a chip. Instead, many companies contribute based on their specific areas of expertise. As a result,

---

[28] Kathleen Walsh, *Foreign High Tech R&D in China* (Washington DC: Stimson Center, 2003), provides a comprehensive political economy analysis of the Chinese software business in the early 2000s.

[29] Pavitt is quoted in Ernst. See note 31 below.

integrated forms of design organization, where almost entire integrated circuits (ICs) are designed within a single firm, are giving way to vertical specialization, where stages of IC design are outsourced (dis-integration of firm organization) and relocated across national boundaries (geographic dispersion). Much of the dis-integrated geographic dispersion is now relocating in China and other Asian economies.

China is also attracting more semiconductor production because of the strides it has made in entering the global market for chip design. It appears that during the "global" downturn in the IT industries in the years 2001–2003, Asia's leading IT exporting countries seized upon new opportunities to create commercially successful innovations in the production of hardware, software, and services, including semiconductors.

Asia, excluding Japan, is the fastest growing market for electronic design automation (EDA) tools. In 2000, Asia's EDA tool market grew 24 percent compared with 6 percent growth in North America, 13 percent in Europe, and 17 percent in Japan. A survey conducted in January 2003 suggests that, excluding Japan, Asia's share in the global production of chip design has increased from practically nothing during the mid 1990s to around 30 percent in 2002; North America's share is 60 percent.[30] By 2008, Asia's share is projected to grow to more than 50 percent. Most of the growth will be in China.

Design complexity is low for a simple, single-layer IC but rises substantially for a multi-layer device. China has carefully but quickly moved up the ladder of complexity in IC design. Combined with the experience in detailed product design and engineering that Asian firms have accumulated in the fabrication of high-precision components like ICs, board-level design has given rise to a broad portfolio of design implementation capabilities. This explains why Asian original design manufacturers (ODMs) like HonHai and Mitac from Taiwan and NamTai from Hong Kong compete successfully with the leading U.S.-controlled global electronic manufacturing services (EMS) providers, like Flextronics and Solectron.[31]

Another enabling factor in rapid development of the Chinese semiconductor business was the emergence of global vendors of design-automation tools, such as Synopsis, Cadence, and Mentor. Application-specific integrated circuit (ASIC) design requires well-defined procedures to develop and use cell libraries that contain design modules. To do this cost-effectively, a new design methodology was developed. The design requirements were implemented in a software language that inscribed digital circuits at the register transfer layer, which is more deeply imbedded in the design of the chip. Access to increasingly sophisticated EDA tools was critical to implementing this new design. As these tools became available on the market, albeit at a very high price, they provided entry opportunities for Asian design companies. And as the effective use of these tools required tweaking and adjustments, Asian companies were able to accumulate a broad set of capabilities related to the implementation of these increasingly automated design methodologies.[32]

---

[30] www.isupply.com
[31] Dieter Ernst, "Complexity and Internationalisation of Innovation—Why is Chip Design Moving to Asia?," East-West Center, Honolulu, Hawaii, forthcoming in *International Journal of Innovation Management*, special issue in honor of Keith Pavitt (Peter Augsdoerfer, Jonathan Sapsed and James Utterback, guest editors)
[32] Ibid.

Three other developments are further accelerating the growth and expanding the scope of IC design in Asia. First, global firms are expanding and upgrading their design centers in Asia as part of their global design networks. Second, leading Asian firms are emerging as new sources of IC design in pursuit of strategies to upgrade system development and standard-setting capabilities, especially in China. Third, smaller Asian firms are attempting to enter global design networks as specialized suppliers, primarily of design implementation services.

In addition, all major global systems companies are expanding their Asian IC design centers to establish their own reference or platform designs as de facto module standards,[33] especially for the next developments, 3G and 4G networks. This reflects the growing importance of Asia as a major growth market for existing IT products and services. In addition, China, Taiwan, and Korea now play leading roles as global test beds and launch markets for innovations in mobile telecommunications and digital consumer systems. This will accelerate as portable Internet devices become more common and eventually ubiquitous.[34]

China's attempt to develop an alternative 3G digital wireless standard, called TD-SCDMA (time division synchronous code-division multiple access) created a strong motivation to expand Asian IC design activities. The TD-SCDMA standard, one of three 3G standards approved by the ITU, was developed by Datang Telecom, a state-owned enterprise (SOE), and the Research Institute of the Ministry of Information Industry (MII), with technical assistance from Siemens. TD-SCDMA has been slow to market, and the Chinese government is holding up 3G licenses until it is ready to compete commercially with other GSM and CDMA standards. The system is expected to enter production soon and may become a standard used more in developing countries, especially if China, as expected, underwrites or subsidizes Chinese suppliers. Nevertheless, the momentum in China created by TD-SCDMA has facilitated in China the creation of the largest and most diverse 3G and 4G test beds in the world. Combined with the other developments noted in this section, it indicates that China will be a key source of wireless products and applications in the future.

Software Development

As noted earlier, telecommunications and IT are inter-related. The term *telecommunications systems* describes the physical infrastructure; the applications and back office functions are provided by IT services. China's software development related to the telecommunications and Internet industries lags behind the United States in a number of significant ways, but it is improving.

Although there is certainly good programming in China, it is still a developing field. As recently as 15 years ago it was impossible to study for a degree in China in software or computer science as independent disciplines. Compared to the United States, India, and Russia, Chinese software companies are small and still generally imitative. Some observers in China also believe that the

---

[33] This refers to packaged software modules that can be sold for re-use in a variety of applications under development.

[34] "The Portable Internet," an ITU Report on the Internet, September 2004.

industry suffered catastrophically in the dot.com and telecommunications collapse of 2000, which lead many promising programmers and developers to seek work outside the telecommunications sector. That the industry has recovered so quickly is evidence of the enormous educational and highly mobile human resources available to Chinese policymakers.

As a strong supporter of the software industry, the government offers incentives that range from tax concessions to research grants. On the other hand, as a regulator, it often makes decisions that restrict access to funds or technologies and tend to restrict the industry's natural growth and progress, especially in areas such as financial system practices and regulations. Internet content development is widely accepted to be closely monitored and controlled. Ultimately, China values order more than market efficiency.

The government has established a series of administrative guidelines that, in effect, give large, SOEs an advantage over their private-sector competitors. These advantages include access to bank financing. In the telecommunications industry, contract applicants for government work must obtain a Certificate of Capability and Quality, issued by the Ministry of Information Industry (MII) at national, provincial, and municipal levels. The standards set for this certificate have nothing to do with projects executed or objective work process considerations, but are based strictly on such traditional measurements as number of engineers, total net assets, registered capital, and annual revenues. In China, it is very difficult for most private-sector companies to meet these requirements.

The main difference between software companies in China and those in developed countries is that few Chinese companies depend on the features of their products for competitive advantage. Competition is based on price, distribution, and relationships. This is beginning to change in the major cities where international business standards are more common, particularly in the eastern coastal regions.

Custom software development and integration shops are numerous and cover the entire range in terms of size, geographic coverage, technical capabilities, and other corporate measures. They tend to be industry-focused and regional. To make inroads into their respective industries, they must have strong domestic relationships with the industry, which can result in technical mediocrity, because purchases are based on measures other than technical merit. Relationships are still primary in China.

Yet, domestic software producers can be competitive with foreign suppliers in several industries, from tax collection to hospital information systems. The language barrier and reluctance of foreign vendors to localize their offerings are strengthening this trend. Domestic products tend to be less expensive and have fewer functions than similar foreign products but are often adequate for the job they are asked to perform. Domestic solutions are often based on open source code that is repackaged for the Chinese market.

Foreign-owned labs in China place much more emphasis on finding product applications for their theoretical findings, following the iterative model described earlier. Researchers are working on computer graphics, speech recognition, text translation, and value-added telecommunications services using interactive voice response.

A conservative estimate is that as many as 300 foreign research centers, mostly software engineering, have been founded in China in the last three years. The Chinese Ministry of Commerce claims 600, with expectations of 200 more per year.[35]

In computer software, Chinese companies such as Founder, Red Flag, UFSoft, Neusoft, Kingdee, and Top Group are both partnering and competing with foreign, high-tech leaders such as Microsoft, Oracle, IBM, and Sun Microsystems.[36] In telecommunications software, Huawei, Zhongxing, Datang Telecom, and Nanjing PTIC are high-tech competitors that are quickly gaining ground in China and in foreign markets against foreign equipment suppliers such as Lucent, Nortel, Alcatel, and Cisco.

Implications

Approximately 86 percent of R&D in global information technology and telecommunications still takes place in industrialized countries, with the United States occupying the lead position with 37 percent. The United States remains ahead in the most prized areas of technological innovation, as far as these can be measured by patent statistics. The U.S. innovation score measures the number of patents granted by the U.S Patent Office, multiplied by an index that incorporates the value of these patents. Since 1985, the U.S. innovation score has more than doubled and far exceeded that of any other country. In 2002, all 15 leading companies with the best records on patent citations were based in the United States. Nine of them were in the IT sector.

But there is evidence of an accelerating strengthening of Asian capability in technological knowledge creation. In a handful of emerging centers of excellence in Asia, sophisticated innovation and research capability appear to have followed the earlier development of electronics manufacturing capability. For the first time, Chinese companies submit and are awarded more patents than foreign joint ventures or wholly foreign-owned enterprises in China. Huawei, which claims to have continuously invested more than 10 percent of its revenues in R&D, states that it now owns 46 Wide-band Code Division Multiple Access (WCDMA) basic patents, accounting for 5 percent of all WCDMA basic patents in the world.

Global macro economic factors also work to Asia's, and especially China's, advantage. As a result of the 2001-2003 downturn in the global IT sector, winning design contracts from global chip set makers has become increasingly difficult and costly for western design houses. This trend reflects the extremely cautious approach of chip set makers to new product development. For IC design, this implies that improving performance features is combined with a relatively conservative approach to design that helps to improve manufacturing yields.

Interviews by Dieter Ernst show that Asian system companies are more willing to use new and unconventional chip designs. Their concern is whether these designs will enable them to reach

---

[35] "Let a Thousand Ideas Flower: China is a New Hotbed of Research",
www.nytimes.com/2004/09/13/technology/13China.html.
[36] See Walsh for a wider assessment of Chinese technological trends.

their main objectives: to improve both speed-to-market and market penetration. This approach sets the Asian system companies apart from the global market leaders, who are more cautious and unwilling to shoulder the higher costs and risks of innovative designs. A shift in the market for more sophisticated and innovative chip sets may provide a further, powerful incentive for more of the large manufacturers and design houses to relocate to the region.

The growth of the low-cost, base software and semiconductor industry in China, which provides the underlying technologies for all telecommunications equipment and applications, has immediate consequences. It permits experimentation in product design and development that will result in new products and services designed, manufactured, and competing in global markets.

PT Expocomm, the largest telecommunications exhibition in China, is held annually at the Beijing International Exhibition Center. Previously the stars of the show were American and European companies, which often invested several hundred thousands of dollars in impressive displays. In October 2004 and 2005, PT Expocomm was primarily a Chinese show. Few American and European companies even bothered to show up. At both shows, the most important in the world's largest telecommunications market, only a handful of American companies exhibited.

The design, quality, and cost of Chinese-produced telecommunications equipment, especially handheld and remote access devices, now equals or surpasses common global standards. Chinese design criteria and advanced manufacturing processes enable Chinese manufacturers to produce a wide variety of products to satisfy individual customer or user requirements. It is important to understand that the newest mobile technologies, which will have military capabilities equal to handheld wireless capabilities used by U.S forces, will mostly be produced in China. Few major American companies compete, at least so far, in this sector of the telecommunications market. Those that claim advanced capabilities almost certainly have a significant portion of their products manufactured in China.

4. Capital and Finance in Chinese Telecommunications

Access to capital is one of the key factors in telecommunications innovation. Until very recently, China's capital markets were undeveloped, and it was very difficult, especially for innovative, entrepreneurial companies, to get funded. This explains to some degree the heavy role in capital allocation played by the Chinese government. The situation remains dire for many promising companies, because government funds often go to politically powerful industry groups. However, success is bringing capital accumulation and more vehicles for funding are quickly becoming available. This will accelerate the rate of technical innovation in China.

Today, internally generated profits—especially from manufacturing export firms—re-invested into product development, are becoming the most important sources of funding for technological innovation. External sources of funds are mainly from local and central government and banks. Equity markets and external equity financing channels, including private equity, play a relatively small but growing role in technological innovation. As the balance changes, corporate foreign direct investment will play a diminishing role.

Private Equity in China

Private equity is used to fund start-up companies as they attempt to introduce new technologies or methods into the marketplace and move toward break even, eventual profitability, and funding through an initial private offering (IPO). Start-ups are high-risk investments in any country and even more so in China, because its recent transition to capital markets is reflected in an underdeveloped corporate legal system. So, in China, money for start-ups usually is not available from lending agencies, such as banks or bond issuers, which depend on stable payments. This means that private equity investors are often the only ones with money to fund entrepreneurial companies,

Private equity investors encounter challenges at every step of the process, including identifying companies to invest in, performing due diligence, negotiating terms, and exiting their investments.

The first problem is finding the deal. Despite its authoritarian, centralized political governance, China is a fractured market. Each region, province, and industry has different regulatory and taxation requirements. The high-tech industry has several geographical zones, each very large and with numerous potential opportunities. Often, accounting is deficient or practices inefficient, making valuation of companies difficult.

The second problem is that negotiating deals is extremely difficult. Chinese entrepreneurs and experienced finance specialists often can't agree on valuations—the price of the investment. Third-world entrepreneurs are notorious for attempting to overvalue their assets, leading to tedious negotiations over unrealistic expectations. Chinese firms often benchmark their valuations based on similar firms in America, while equity firms and private investors stress the different risk factors.

The third problem, which is related to the second, is that national growth rates are a factor in valuation. Valuations for Chinese firms may be boosted disproportionately by China's overall growth prospects.

Gaining control can be difficult, and Chinese entrepreneurs are unyielding. Even in larger companies, major investors find it difficult to gain board seats, and minority shareholder rights are widely ignored.

Another problem is finding and keeping a strong management team. Many Chinese managers, especially those who speak English and work for foreign companies, change jobs frequently for higher pay.

Finally, channels for exiting an investment are narrow. The Shanghai and Shenzen stock markets almost exclusively list SOEs. Chinese firms often look for strategic buyers to provide liquidity—typically foreign corporations looking to acquire new capabilities or the opportunity to snap up smaller, innovative firms. Hong Kong and New York stock markets are much more open to IPOs than are Chinese stock markets.

Private equity investors have been cautious about investing in China. Even in developed countries there is very little legal redress for private equity losses, but money lost in China is truly money lost. As the legal system develops to protect investors, there is more interest in private investment in China. Historically, the level or amount of private equity invested in a country or industry has been a leading indicator of innovation. So far, most American venture capital firms have done no more than a handful of deals in China.[37]

Today, most capital in China is from internal sources, though this is changing. According to the *China Business Review*, "China is the most important growth market for private equity in Asia."[38] But China's financial markets and major banking companies are poorly equipped to fund its growth. Chinese banks loan much of their money to SOEs and lack the credit tools to analyze the credit risk of new firms with unproven technology.

In fact, it may be easier today for Chinese high-tech startups to get funded by American funding companies, especially private equity firms, than it is for American start-ups. Investment is a herd activity. The sense among private investors today is that China is the place to be, the center of future capital growth, and that the American economy is in decline, especially in high-tech, communications related businesses. Twenty-five percent of high-tech IPOs on Wall Street in 2004 were Chinese companies. And indeed there is an intensity of activity in current Chinese telecommunications development that is not as apparent in the United States.

---

[37] *Business Week*, June 14, 2004
[38] "Private Equity in China: Risk for Reward," *The China Business Review*, July-August 2004, pg.48.

Despite China's clear lead in attracting foreign direct investment, for example corporate investment in developing new subsidiaries, India attracted more private equity annually until 2003. India's predictable laws, multiple stock exchanges, and recent entrepreneurial history are a strong draw. But global investment firms are reacting positively to new Chinese regulations and perceived openness to private business. According to the *Asian Venture Capital Review*, China attracted $1.3 billion in private equity in 2004, 30 percent more than in 2003. As much as $1 billion of that capital was in the form of venture capital. Carlyle Asian Ventures, for example, is planning to invest between $750 million and $1 billion in China in the next two years.

Private equity investors are directing their capital to three categories: first, to the hundreds of SOEs that are selling, restructuring, or privatizing parts of their assets; second, to established private businesses, which typically manufacture for domestic and international supply chains; third, to entrepreneurial start-ups in information technology, telecommunications, and biotechnology.

Corporate Investment

China remains a favorite destination of corporate capital investment. Actual foreign direct investment (FDI) rose to nearly $60 billion in 2004. Contracted FDI, deals that are signed but not yet completed, jumped even higher, to $73 billion in the same period.[39]

However, FDI figures deserve closer analysis. In the late 1990s, actual and contracted FDI numbers matched as firms invested as fast as they could sign deals. Although the absolute sums have grown, a gap has emerged and widened. Not all the deals that are signed materialize, evidence that an increasing number are turning sour.

There are foreign companies making good money in China, but the business environment is difficult for foreigners. Navigating China's opaque bureaucracies and maze of ever-changing rules, finding trustworthy local partners, understanding that Chinese officials at the highest levels demand much but offer little in return for their support, and battling piracy and outright fraud continue to take up more time, energy, and money than in any other major market.

The growing spread between signed deals and actual investment can mean two things. One is that foreign companies are tired of losing money in a country that only wants their money to develop its own economy and places structural barriers to earning revenues in China. Another is that the Chinese government departments that approve the deals are becoming more selective. As their own high-tech companies become competitive internationally in a particular sector, there is less need for foreign funding or technology transfer in that sector. Increasingly, the only plans and deals authorized are those that fill technical gaps and facilitate the ability of the Chinese industrial sector to compete internationally. The Chinese government plays a mercantilist, zero-sum game.

---

[39] "Fools Rush In," *The Economist*, August 7, 2004, pg.50.

Problems of Capital and Innovation

Chinese technocrats and financial specialists dealing in corporate finance are still struggling with the requirement of transitioning from a tightly controlled, command economy to a predominantly market economy. Firms have to distribute R&D capital carefully to obtain the correct balance of imported and indigenous technology. This supports the well-known Chinese innovation model of imitation-improvement-innovation. When companies have adequate capital accumulation, which many now have, then they can support indigenous R&D directed at indigenous innovation. [40]

Financing technical innovation in China is cumbersome and complex. China, like all major economies, is struggling to understand the best ways that government and private investment can spur innovation. There are five core issues facing China in financing innovation. [41]

- Most funding for technology development in the phase between invention and innovation comes from corporations, the Beijing central ministries, and a small but growing number of wealthy private equity investors—not venture capitalists. The issue remains one of transparency into the innovative process and accounting practices.

- Markets for allocating risk capital to early-stage technology ventures are not efficient.

- Despite market inefficiencies, many institutional arrangements have developed for funding early-stage technology development. Funding mechanisms have evolved to match the incentives and motivations of entrepreneurs and investors; there is a lot of cross investment among companies in the same industry group, much like the Japanese *keiretsu*, Sumitomo, Itochu, and Mitsubishi .

- The conditions for success in science-based, high-tech innovation are concentrated in a few geographical regions, indicating the importance in this process of innovation-investor proximity and networks of supporting people and institutions. These areas include Shanghai-Hangzhou-Suzhou; Taiwan-Shenzen-Guangzhou; Beijing (Haidian)-Tianjin.

- Only a fraction of R&D spending in corporations is dedicated to early-stage technology development, though the amount varies among firms and within industries.

Taken together the current state of funding, which lacks flexibility, can lead to mistakes in product development. In the middle 1990's many telecommunication manufacturers in China assumed that the router market was owned worldwide by Cisco and there was no point in competing against them. Huawei, with access to large amounts of government funding, has

---

[40] "Financial Performance of Technical Innovation in China," Prof Jian Gao. A three-part study of the structure of financial sources and performance of technological innovation in China, U.S.-China Seminar on Technical Innovations, George Mason University, May 2004.
[41] Ibid.

proved that this was an error by competing effectively against Cisco, particularly in developing countries.

Chapter Summary

Many promising Chinese technical companies have problems raising money, especially small and mid-size entrepreneurial once that are often the source of new ideas. However, there are changes taking place that will facilitate innovation. In 2002, a collection of private equity firms founded the China Venture Capital Association to boost bargaining power and promote entrepreneurial rights. Its fifty members include such leading investment companies as Carlyle, Newbridge Capital, and Goldman Sachs. In January 2003, the PRC clarified the Venture Capital Regulations, which are rules governing private equity investments.[42] Those changes promote investment in high technology and address issues of capital formation, capital contribution, and application procedures. In addition, investors are optimistic that the gradual emergence of a professional managerial class will help private equity firms build new businesses.

Loosening capital controls and easing the ability of foreign investors to repatriate profits would be welcome changes for foreign investors and would accelerate Chinese innovation. Also, loosening listing requirements for IPOs for small- and medium-size companies will provide capital for growing companies and create new exit opportunities for private investors.

---

[42] *China Business Review*, July-August 2004. p.24

5. A Potential Leapfrog Technology? IPv6 as a New Model of Chinese Technical Leadership

IPv6 Defined[43]

IPv6 stands for Internet Protocol version 6. The Internet has been using IP version 4 for addressing since it was invented. Eventually, all IPv4 domain addresses will be in use. The problem is considered serious in China, which was allocated relatively few IPv4 addresses.

IPv6 will allow expansion beyond the current limitation of four billion addresses to a number that approaches infinity in our current understanding of networked technologies. IPv6 functionally determines the addressing schemes and hierarchies of the next generation Internet

IPv6 also allows for greater inherent security, as well as improved support for mobile users and wireless devices, which is where almost all telecommunications and Internet product manufacturing and services growth is centered.

Why is IPv6 Important?

The importance of IPv6 goes far beyond mere technological advantage, especially in China.

- It has an expanded addressing scheme that permits several different levels of security. The impact of individual levels of security within IPv6 probably is known, but not the impacts of security elements used in diverse combinations. So it is possible that a country that assumes leadership in this technology may find new ways to provide security and encryption that will give it competitive, strategic, and tactical advantages. This is one of the few ways that a country could achieve telecommunications dominance today.

- As noted in section one, John Gage, Sun Microsystems Chief Technology Officer, sees China as an intellectual Internet cauldron. The atmosphere in China resembles that of the San Francisco Bay area during the PC revolution of the early 1980s. By the end of this decade, with perhaps 50 million technicians, support specialists, and university level IT-educated, ardent, and explorative users under the age of 30 experimenting with IPv6, important innovations are likely to emerge.

---

[43] An excellent introduction to the technical and network complexities of IPv6 is available in Clay Wilson, "Network Centric Warfare: Background and Oversight Issues for Congress, Appendix A, CRS Report for Congress, Mar 18, 2005.

- IPv6 provides the basis to interconnect so many new technologies, even mundane technologies like refrigerators and home lighting systems, that it could permeate a society in ways that are beyond our current political and social understanding.

- IPv6 may be more than a simple technology. It may be a melding of technology and social systems, used to create more controls or used to undermine those imposing controls. In China, IPv6 may be a social utilitarian technology that can meld Chinese political life together in a way IPv4 could not because of its address limitations.

- IPv6 is a source technology of what the ITU describes now as the Portable Internet, the next stage in Internet development. The Portable Internet can level the field in a variety of telecommunications services that provide the backbone for numerous corporate and industrial processes.

- Taking the lead in IPv6 also is consistent with China's long-range plans for technical leadership in standards development and manufacturing. Virtually all the worldwide manufacturing of portable Internet products will be in China.

Innovation in the *social forms of production*—which include, inter alia, trade, education, and the social and geographic distribution of wealth—are just as important as innovations in the material forces of production.[44] Within the international telecommunications industry, IPv6 may develop into something new—a set of products and services that eventually develops into a ubiquitous and technologically convergent social mesh, especially in major business centers like the Chaoyang District of Beijing or the Bay Area of San Francisco and San Jose.

American-Chinese Competition in IPv6

The Chinese government has identified IPv6 as a foundation technology of Chinese Internet expansion and manufacturing supremacy. In the United States, the Department of Defense is the leading proponent for IPv6; there is only limited interest in IPv6 for commercial applications. In China, there seems to be a government and telecommunications industry commitment to the technology as a basis for building both a strong internal network and a robust export capability. Is a battle brewing in the social forms of production between the American defense industry and the Chinese commercial telecommunications industry for primacy in IPv6 and next generation networks?

China and IPv6
According to We Hequan, Vice President of the Chinese Academy of Engineering,[45] the Chinese government is on track to build one the world's largest native IPv6 networks by the end of 2005

---

[44] See Hugill on the relationship between global trade, telecommunications, and perceptions of power.

[45] IPv6 Summit, Beijing, March 2004. IPv6 summits are sponsored by the IPv6 Forum and commercial enterprises and are held in several cities worldwide each year; China and the United States hold annual summits. The purpose is to discuss standards development, products, and general acceptance of the protocol. See www.ipv6.net.cn/summit/2005/index_en.jsp.

and to conduct application trials in an attempt to realize the construction of the first next generation network and next generation Internet in an integrated manner

The term *next generation Internet* (NGI) usually refers to upgrading the current Internet with improved security, quality of service (QoS),[46] convenience, and manageability. The term *next generation network* (NGN) comes from the telephone world and also concerns scalability, mobility, manageability, and QoS. Moving to Internet protocol from time division multiplexing (TDM), the current technical protocol of the telephone industry, is a clear objective for NGN and is well underway. Voice over IP (VoIP) has already surpassed TDM for domestic long distance communications in China in numbers and minutes of calls wherever VOIP telephony is available.

The Chinese government has conducted trials on NGI and NGN separately but intends to merge the two. The large-scale IPv6 test network currently in development in China will be used for interoperability testing of connected devices, as well as for developing mechanisms for QoS, security, and accounting.

In 2003, eight Chinese government ministries, including the National Development and Reform Commission (NDRC), MII, Ministry of Science and Technology, and Ministry of Education, launched the China Next Generation Internet Project (CNGI) to start construction of IPv6 networks. As part of the project, the China Education and Research Network (CERNET) and five telecom carriers were put in charge of building six national IPv6 backbone networks covering 39 areas in China by the end of 2005. These networks will ultimately be linked together and serve as the basic infrastructure for future IPv6 networks.[47]

In addition to CNGI, the MII also launched the IPv6 Telecom Trial Network (6TNet) in May 2002 for application and service trials and for eventually rolling out commercial services. Testing based on the 6TNet is designed to permit telecom operators to come up with commercially viable services and applications, such as video conferencing, VoIP, and presence-location services. The 6TNet is also being used for the testing of IPv6 equipment, on which the approval and issue of sales licenses are based.

For domestic Chinese vendors, early entry into the IPv6 market and development of IPv6 equipment opens up the possibility of setting standards and profiting from royalty payments. The Chinese government will support domestic vendors in setting standards and will give them priority for equipment purchases.

The Chinese government has made limited investments in CNGI and sponsors such events as the annual Global IPv6 Forum in Beijing. An estimated $150 million has been spent by the Chinese government on IPv6 trial equipment, and this is expected to increase dramatically as large-scale test networks are populated by IPv6 routers and servers. BDA, a research firm based in Beijing,

---

[46] Quality of service in telecommunications networking has come to mean the ability to classify different services according to priority and the importance of reducing latency across a network. For example, a voice call gets a higher priority than a data call, because packets must arrive in close sequence for voice over IP to be intelligible. A data stream for, say, a spreadsheet can take longer to get to its destination, though the difference is in milliseconds,
[47] BDA China Ltd., Fang Meiqin, May 31, 2004.

believes that IPv6 routers will become the majority of new installations in China beginning in 2006.

With the IPv6 market expected to grow significantly in the near future, domestic vendors like Huawei, ZTE, Harbour Networks, and Tsinghua Bitway have all started R&D on the technology. Huawei is the most aggressive and claims in sales literature that all of its routers support IPv6 by mid 2004. In Telecom Expo 2005 in Beijing in October 2005 it was clear that IPv6 was a major marketing and technical aspect of both the conference and product exhibitions from virtually all the major telecommunication designers and manufacturers in China.

The United States and IPv6
The United States does not have a national telecommunications policy explicitly focused on IPv6, but the United States government has promoted the concept for several years. John Osterholz, then-director of the DOD Office of Architecture and Interoperability, told the IPv6 Summit in June 2003 that DOD would phase out purchases of IPv4 network technologies by autumn and begin trials of equipment and applications based on IPv6 for the Internet. This is consistent with the building of the Global Information Grid (GIG), which is meant to be a fully distributed, available, and secure network to support warfighting abroad and ensure homeland security.

Plans were outlined for moving the entire DOD IT infrastructure—the world's largest with an annual budget exceeding $30 billion—into IPv6 compliance by 2008. Such a change, based on the expectations of a particular technological development, required a broad-based change in procurement practices. Virtually the entire commercial Internet infrastructure, which includes IPv6 summit attendees Cisco, HP, Nokia, and the Verio division of NTT Japan, was provided with detailed specifications on the networking standards DOD plans to support.

Historically, DOD commissioned vendors to build proprietary infrastructure. But the DOD need for immediate, global access to secure, real-time information has moved the requirement from an infrastructure of data links between proprietary systems to a global network built on the next generation of open systems, which is an underlying foundation of the GIG.

However, many U.S. manufacturing and services providers see only a marginally compelling reason to make an early move to IPv6. They invested heavily in IPv4 infrastructure and want to see returns on this investment before moving forward with a new technology. This means that IPv6 development in the United States, driven only by DOD, may be slow. A future can be envisioned where much of what is planned for the GIG will be manufactured and tested in China before it is sold to DOD by U.S. based vendors.

Testimony at Congressional hearings in June 2005 indicates that the Department of Defense is proceeding cautiously with IPv6. IPv6 capability is mandated for purchase of new equipment, but IPv6 technology is not now used in tactical systems. Significant interoperability testing is required and underway. IPv6 will be implemented as budgets and mission requirements permit.[48]

---

[48] Statement by George G Wauer, Director, Architecture and Interoperability, Office of the Assistant Secretary of Defense for Networks and Information Integration and DOD Chief Information Officer, before the House Committee on Government Reform, June 29, 2005.

At the IPv6 summit in Reston, VA, in early December 2005, it was reported that mid-level government IT specialists were still indicating a lack of senior leadership direction in IPv6 implementation.[49]

Chapter Summary

Great care must be taken not to exaggerate any particular technical development and assign to it qualities it does not possess. American software designers were leaders in the development of the IPv6 protocols, and many of the software modules used in IPv6 products in China currently are licensed from U.S. companies. However, the history of Chinese technological suggests that this will change. Chinese companies will follow their standard model of technical development: license, imitate, incrementally improve, and finally innovate in IPv6 product development.

The strategic concern is different than anything the United States has faced before. IPv6 is a political and social phenomenon in China. Up to now, China has been generally imitative. IPv6 is the first techno-intellectual platform that will permit the hundreds of thousands of engineers and software designers educated and being educated in China to develop sets of their own products on what is becoming a global foundation of telecommunications technology and protocol.

Given the U.S. emphasis on military applications, IPv6 is one area where military competition between China and the United States is likely.

---

[49] See www.usipv6.com for reports on the conference.

6. Tentative Conclusions: Strategic Geopolitics of the International Telecommunications System

New Conceptions of Strategy

This paper argues that the international telecommunications system is in transition from U.S. dominance to distributed, regional dominance. While India and Russia have great potential, China will be the greatest regional competitor to U.S. interests. China's telecommunications rise has many important economic, social, and political implications for the United States. Among these is the need for the Defense Department to carefully consider both how it assesses Chinese capabilities and how it plans to use telecommunications networks in the future.

The perception that the United States is still the global telecommunications leader is dangerous insofar as U.S. defense planners fail to accurately assess China's future military capabilities. With the ability to collect and share information a vital part of any modern military, China's capacity to improve the PLA in this area must be considered. Yet, most recent writing on China and the PLA still analyzes China's hard-asset defense industries. A good example of this genre, and a well-produced and thoughtful article in its issue area, was published by John Frankenstein for The Atlantic Council in early 2003. According to Frankenstein, when the People's Republic of China was established in 1949, its economy and industrial base was demolished, yet within twenty years the Chinese defense industrial complex (CDIC) was producing a full range of relatively modern military equipment, including strategic weapons. But the sector did not keep pace with modernization, and today is regarded as an industrial dinosaur, unable to achieve that most meaningful metric in this era of economic reform, profitability. More importantly, the CDIC has not been able to design and produce the systems the Chinese military deems necessary in future, with the result that China has become dependent on foreign sources for key technologies and weapons system. The Chinese are not unaware of CDIC shortcomings, but the various attempts to resolve the sector's problems—reorganization and "conversion"—have been only marginally successful. [50] The assumption is that China remains behind the U.S. in important military technologies.

What this line of thinking doesn't consider fully, and what this paper has stressed throughout, is that the foundations of Chinese strategic capabilities are changing dramatically, and that China and other countries are in the process of taking the lead in several technologies that are critical to telecommunications-based warfare. Key telecommunications technologies for warfare are outside the CDIC, though closely allied with it, but the arms-length distance has enabled the high-tech telecommunications sector to advance with much less bureaucratic interference, and the success is obvious at any large Chinese telecommunications exhibition.[51]

---

[50] "Globalization of Defense Industries: China", John Frankenstein, The Atlantic Council, Occasional Publications Series, Feb. 2003

[51] James Mulvenon and Andrew N.D. Yang, eds. "The People's Liberation Army in the Information Age," RAND Corporation, 1999.

This success will find its way into the military. Since the late 1970s, Chinese leaders have believed that a broad-based modernization of the whole economy will sustain long-term military modernization. During the 16th Party Congress in 2002, China's leaders reaffirmed their primary commitment to economic development and continued support for military modernization. In practice, this translates into the intersection of civilian and military technical development. For example, the Chinese Academy of Sciences conducts research with various institutions on engineering, remote sensing, semiconductors, and lasers throughout China in cities with a strong defense industrial base. As a result, there is close collaboration with the military on "applied research with products funded or developed for use by the military."[52]

Vulnerabilities in Telecommunications and Network Warfare

While sizing up China's growing telecommunications capabilities, U.S. defense leaders must also consider what vulnerabilities this rise creates in their own plans. Telecommunications are a crucial part of the transformation of U.S. forces, especially to the degree that they will operate in a network-centric manner. Network-centric warfare (NCW) puts an especially high premium on the ability of the entire force, from individuals to divisions, to communicate quickly and securely. The diffusion of telecommunications capabilities, and especially China's progress and potential in this area, has created two sorts of vulnerabilities. First, several components of NCW are subject to threat, especially at the physical layer of cables, co-location facilities, and software. Secondly, DOD may soon be in a position of relying on other nations, including China, a potential adversary, to supply technology and equipment that is vital to modern warfighting.

The Internet and what is described as the global telecommunications network are meta-concepts. The terms are convenient shorthand, but in fact there are no such unitary edifices. The global telecommunications network certainly has worldwide applications, but it consists of a web of private networks with strong national ownership. These private, independent networks are increasingly national and regional as the largest telecommunications companies retreat to protect their home markets in an era of unregulated competition. Some planning scenarios for NCW ignore the fact that the network relies on a fragile, international, physical infrastructure that is almost completely beyond the control of U.S. military authorities. In telecommunications-based warfare, where the battlespace includes the international telecommunications network, traditional military tactics become dependent on the switches, routers, and software algorithms that provide direction and intelligence. When the technology and software algorithms belong to China or India, the rules of the game change. This obvious fact is not understood very well, or perhaps is just not acknowledged.

The emerging reliance on international networks in military operations should thus be considered very carefully. The United States no longer has control of the international telecommunications system in any essential or meaningful way, especially outside the continental United States. The United States only has the use of the international telecommunications network for military

---

[52] "Annual Report on the Military Power of the Peoples Republic of China," (Washington, DC: Office of the Secretary of Defense, July 28, 2003)14. Available at http://www.defenselink mil/ news/Jun2000/china06222000 htm

purposes in any country at the pleasure of the host government. Most DOD traffic crosses other national networks, including those of every potential adversary. Foreign nationals control U.S. military information once it leaves the United States. Substantial amounts of U.S.-origin traffic for Asia passes through nodes in Shanghai, Hong Kong, and other facilities in Asia owned by Chinese or Chinese-invested companies. The same is true in the Middle East or Europe. Critical U.S. military traffic may be safe in the sense that it is encrypted, but it can be blocked by other countries that control much of the routing infrastructure.

Telecommunications-based strategies thus rest on a fragile infrastructure that can be crashed by anyone with a serious intention to do so. Not only can national governments deny their networks to U.S. use, but vulnerable network points are easily located and destroyed by any reasonably informed terrorist organization, and certainly by any state adversary with its own telecommunications infrastructure. Chinese and Indian computer experts, among others, understand this and most likely have the know-how to control traffic patterns in an escalatory process geared to political goals.

A second major area of network vulnerability is that the diffusion of telecommunications capabilities raises the prospect U.S. military operations will depend on foreign-manufactured equipment at the end of foreign-managed circuits run by foreign contract engineers. It is reported that U.S. Department of Defense planners are buying dark fiber and secure collocation facilities and hiring contract workers overseas to manage the GIG. However, dark fibers are unlit circuits on the same cables everyone else uses; there is no such thing as a secure collocation facility anywhere, including the United States, and one cannot really expect a foreign national to be loyal to the United States if the host country turns into a competitor or adversary, or decides it does not want to participate in a particular action.

Much of the equipment and software that supports telecommunications-based military operations is based on open systems. All potential adversaries have the same equipment and operating systems. Unless trends change dramatically, most of the equipment for telecommunications-based warfare is produced in Asia, especially China, under contract to U.S. companies that increasingly are manufacturers in name only. The leading American companies selling NCW equipment and services are, increasingly, the assemblers and sales distribution channels of Chinese manufacturers.

Conclusion

American conceptions of telecommunications-based warfare have been conditioned by the belief that the United States is the leader in networking and telecommunications technologies. If the United States retains the lead today, that lead is narrow and may disappear, even if the United States puts massive resources into staying ahead. This outcome will be a function of human resources and capital. Europe, China, and India together massively outweigh the United States in human potential and capital resources. Many of the technologies developed by these countries are at least as good as those designed and manufactured by American companies (think 3G). And they are unquestionably dual-use technologies.

The world is much more balanced economically and technically than is supposed or acknowledged. Many countries now have sufficient asymmetric capabilities to constrain U.S. telecommunications-based warfare in a strategic crisis, simply by exercising their ownership prerogatives of turning the system off or redirecting traffic. With regard to China, the question, "How is China responding to American military transformation?" misses the point. China is responding in every way—science, technology, education, new approaches to military officer training, capital allocation, etc. China has systematically used a mercantilist economic and regulatory policy to acquire the predominant position in the global production of network equipment—the routers, the wireless technologies, and the microprocessor technologies that underpin them.

Global telecommunications is no longer the monopoly of any one country. American defense policies will have to adjust to this profound change in the strategic environment.